VALENTINA GOTTARDI, MACIEJ MICHNO and DANIO MISEROCCHI

THE TOMORROW TREE

How Nature Creates New Life From Old

CONTENTS

- 4   The second life of trees
- 6   Insects
- 10   Mosses and lichens
- 12   Fungi and molluscs
- 16   Small mammals and birds
- 20   Snow
- 24   Forest flowers
- 28   Large animals
- 34   The forest and us
- 36   Messy is best
- 37   Glossary*
- 38   New life from dead wood

*You can find the words in **bold** in the glossary.

THE SECOND LIFE OF TREES

In every forest, sooner or later, a new clearing will be created by a falling tree. The tree may be blown down by the wind. It may be struck by lightning. After falling, these once proud giants are left on the ground to rot.

'How sad,' we might think.

But for the forest, the death of a tree is not a loss. A fallen tree is a new beginning. Think of a dead tree as a 'tomorrow tree'. It will be a future home, as well as food, for many things in the forest. Every part of the tree will be used. Its wood will provide places to feed, thrive and create new life. Animals and plants will benefit. **Fungi**, **bacteria** and many other **organisms** will, too.

A large fallen tree will become a home for many species. Some might live there for a long time (sometimes more than thirty years!). The tree will also greatly increase the different kinds of species found in the area. This is known as an area's 'biodiversity'.

A fallen tree will become a space where stories of life, both great and small, will unfold.

A. STAG BEETLE LARVAE
Lucanus cervus
Larvae are young insects. These ones live near the roots.

B. CARPENTER ANT
Camponotus ligniperda
These ants carve out their nest into the dead wood.

C. BEECH BARK BEETLE
Taphrorychus bicolor
These beetles chew tunnels under the bark. The tunnels form patterns.

INSECTS

A beech tree has fallen in a forest in Europe. Its roots were partly rotten and its grip on the ground was weak. A burst of wind has uprooted it. Now it lies in a clearing, warmed by the summer sun.

Stag beetle larvae were already living among its rotting roots. Little has changed for them. They go on with their lives surrounded by **fungi**. The fungi help to **decompose** the dead wood they feast on.

The warm tree trunk attracts alpine longhorn beetles. These blue-grey insects explore the bark and feed on the wood.

Carpenter ants are giants compared with other ants. Like the beetles, these big ants are drawn to the tree. They build complex nests in the decaying trunk. They do this by carving out passages in the wood.

Over time the bark peels away. This reveals tunnels made by beech bark beetles. Females of this species burrow into the wood. As they go, they lay eggs. Soon, young beetles hatch. After hatching, the tiny larvae continue to tunnel into the trunk. As they feed, they create patterns. This makes room for their partners, fungi.

This fallen tree provides homes, food and safety. It is even a playground for the young of different species. It is not just 'dead wood'.

Anatomy of a stag beetle

The stag beetle belongs to the order of insects called Coleoptera. This is the scientific name for beetles. This order also includes ladybirds. There are at least 350,000 other types of beetle.

Beetles have two pairs of wings. They do not use the top pair to fly. These wings are hard, like armour. They protect the second pair of wings and the abdomen. Each wing is known as an elytron. Together they are called elytra.

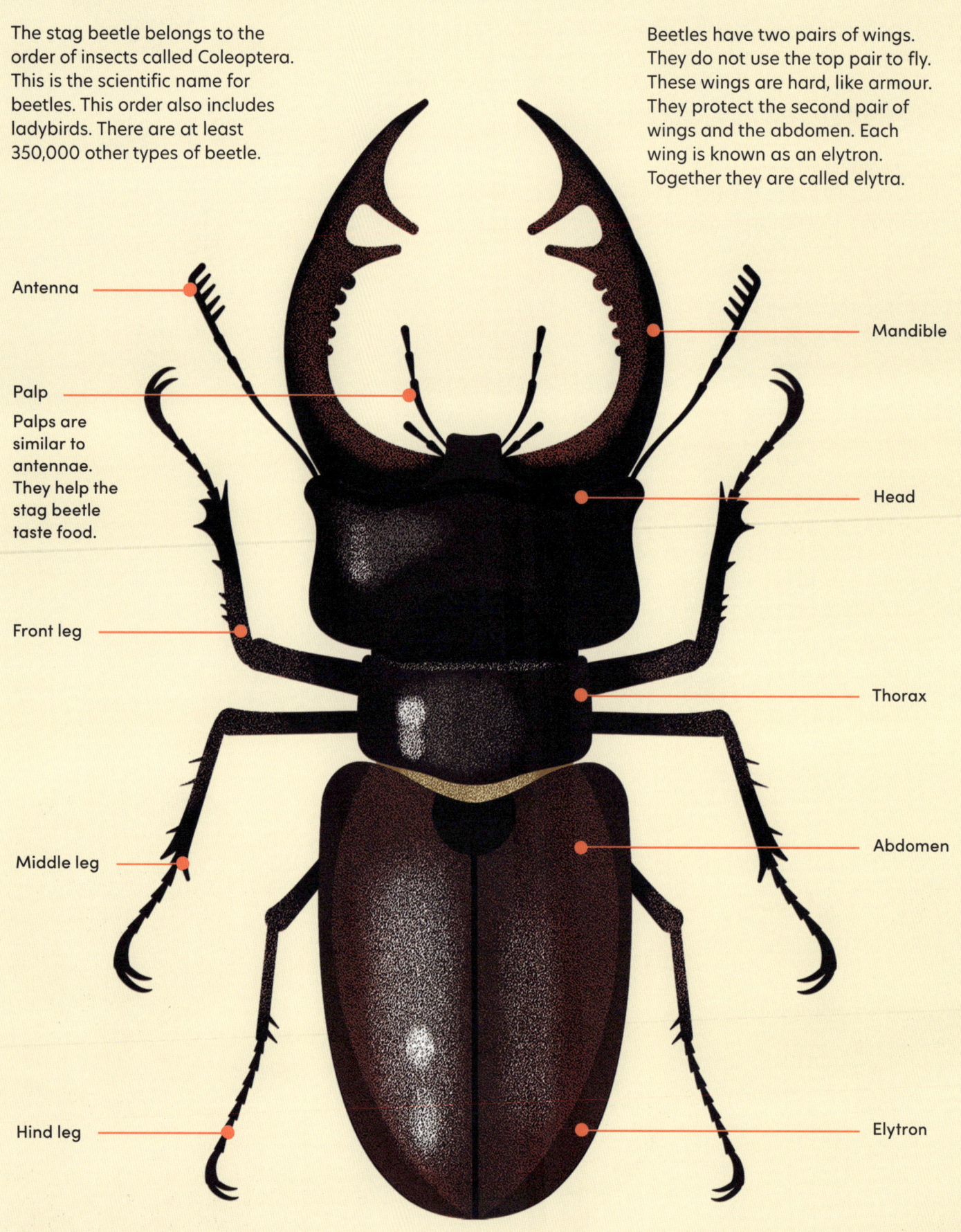

- Antenna
- Palp
- Palps are similar to antennae. They help the stag beetle taste food.
- Front leg
- Middle leg
- Hind leg
- Mandible
- Head
- Thorax
- Abdomen
- Elytron

ALPINE LONGHORN BEETLE
Rosalia alpina
The alpine longhorn beetle is blue-grey with black spots. This helps to perfectly camouflage it against the bark of a beech tree. It likes dead tree trunks that get lots of sunlight. It prefers those that are still standing.

SPOTTED SNAKE FLY
Phaeostigma notata
This is neither a fly nor a snake. Instead, this insect has a long neck that resembles a snake about to strike. When young, it hunts prey on and under the bark of trees. Adults prefer the foliage, or leaves. In the foliage, they feed on small insects.

CARPENTER ANT
Camponotus ligniperda
Carpenter ants like cool, rainy habitats. They like to build large, complex nests in the damp wood of dead trees. Woodpeckers and bears enjoy eating them.

A CLADONIA
Cladonia sp.
Cladonia is a type of **lichen**. (See opposite page). It forms a green-grey crust or powder on tree trunks. There are several species of *Cladonia*. Each is different. Some even form little cups.

B BIG SHAGGY-MOSS
Rhytidiadelphus triquetrus
This moss grows on fallen trees. It also grows at the bottom of living trees.

C PLANT LITTER
Plant litter carpets the forest floor. It is made from dry leaves, dead wood and other rotted plant bits. These include flowers, seeds and pods. **Fungi** and **bacteria** transform plant litter into fertile soil. This soil is known as **humus**.

MOSSES AND LICHENS

Take a look at the bark of a tree. You may find an **organism** called lichen. Lichen is made up of two living things: an **alga** and a fungus. An alga is a small plant that provides food for the fungus. The fungus, in turn, protects the alga. It also provides the alga with water and minerals. In these ways, lichen's alga and fungus support each other. This is called living in **symbiosis**.

Lichens reproduce when a small part breaks off and grows into a new lichen. The fungal part of lichens can also make spores. Spores are similar to tiny seeds. These can be blown far away by the wind to land in a new home. But to make a new lichen, the spore must find an alga. Once it does, the spore and an alga can then combine to form a new lichen.

Mosses are very small plants that grow in moist, shady places. Like lichen, they grow well on fallen trees. This is because plant litter on the ground acts like a sponge. It holds moisture from rain and dew for a long time.

Lichens and mosses are not **parasites**. Unlike parasites, they do not harm the trees on which they live.

FUNGI AND MOLLUSCS

The trunk and roots of our fallen tree are rich in **fungi** and **bacteria**. So is the moist soil surrounding it. Fungi and bacteria gradually transform the fallen tree and plant litter into **humus**. This fertile soil is a valuable source of plant nutrition. Nothing is wasted. Every leaf, twig and piece of bark is broken down and reused. This means that the forest's cycle of life continues.

Fungi are neither plants nor animals. They are **organisms** largely made up of root-like strands. The strands are called hyphae. These hyphae form a large underground web. This web connects to the roots of nearby trees. It links the forest's plants together.

What is a mushroom?

If you look at the forest floor, you might see a mushroom. A mushroom is actually part of a fungus. It's the part we can see above ground. Picture an apple tree. What if the trunk and branches were under the ground? Imagine we could only see the apples. Mushrooms are like these apples.

The mushroom is called a fungi's 'fruiting body'. It makes tiny spores. These play the same role as seeds. The spores let the fungi spread.

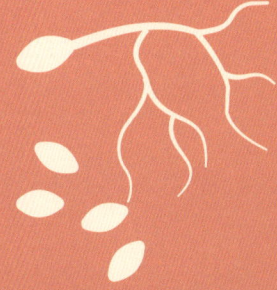

Ⓐ BLUSHING ROSETTE FUNGUS
Abortiporus biennis
This fungus grows on rotten tree stumps. Its shape and colour can resemble a flower.

Ⓑ WRINKLED PEACH MUSHROOM
Rhodotus palmatus
This spectacular mushroom is worth finding on dead trees. Sadly, it is disappearing from forests, which makes it rare to find.

Ⓒ YELLOW CURTAIN CRUST
Stereum insignitum
This fungus has different-coloured rings. During dry weather it dries out. It softens and regains its colour when the rains return.

Ⓓ DEAD MAN'S FINGERS
Xylaria polymorpha
This fungus is scary! It looks like a small hand poking out of an old tree stump.

LEOPARD SLUG
Limax maximus
Slugs like to feed on mushrooms. They are a type of mollusc. Unlike snails, they don't have a shell. There are many species of slug. This one gets its name from the leopard-like pattern on its skin.

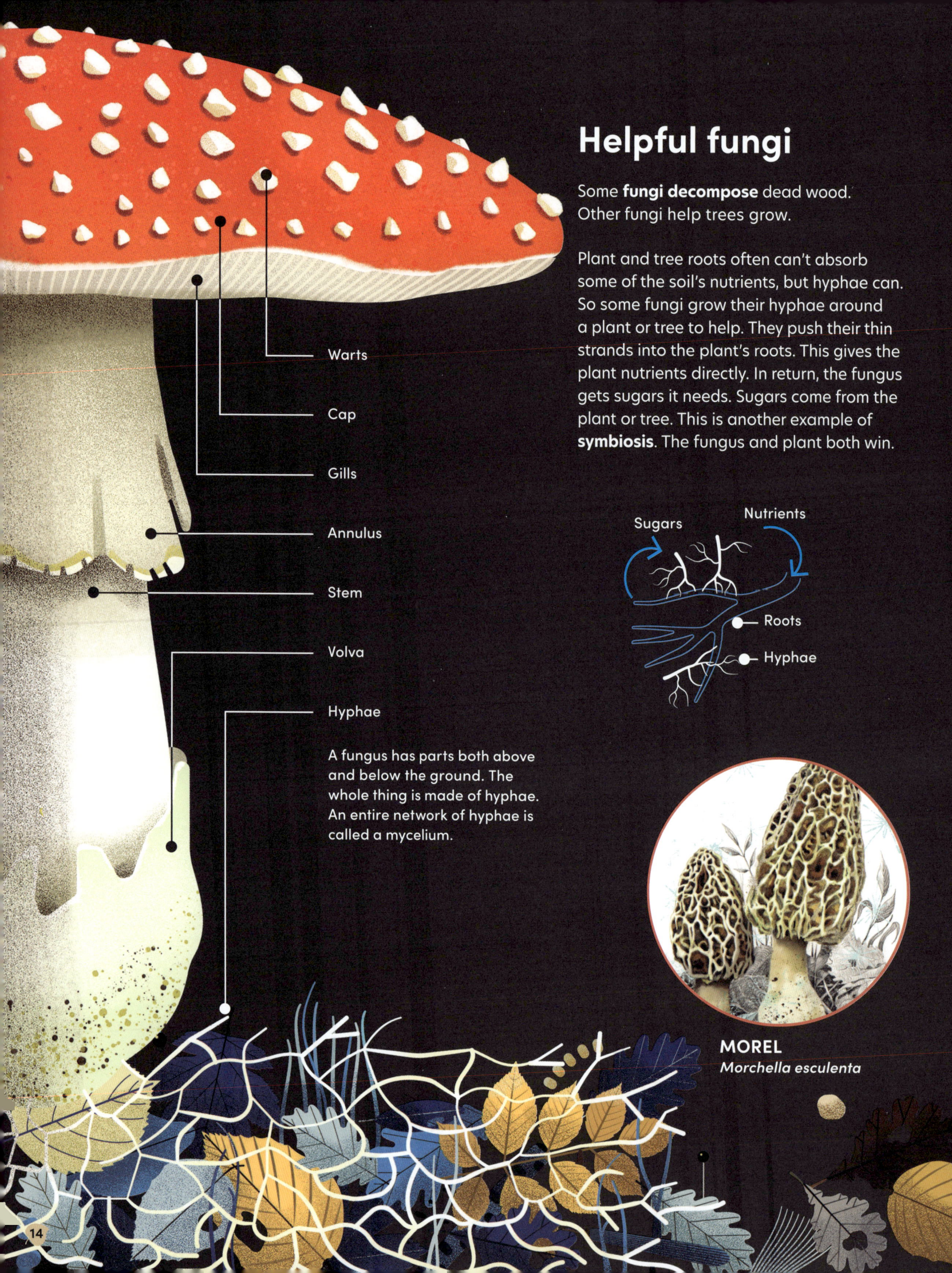

- Warts
- Cap
- Gills
- Annulus
- Stem
- Volva
- Hyphae

A fungus has parts both above and below the ground. The whole thing is made of hyphae. An entire network of hyphae is called a mycelium.

Helpful fungi

Some **fungi decompose** dead wood. Other fungi help trees grow.

Plant and tree roots often can't absorb some of the soil's nutrients, but hyphae can. So some fungi grow their hyphae around a plant or tree to help. They push their thin strands into the plant's roots. This gives the plant nutrients directly. In return, the fungus gets sugars it needs. Sugars come from the plant or tree. This is another example of **symbiosis**. The fungus and plant both win.

Sugars • Nutrients • Roots • Hyphae

MOREL
Morchella esculenta

Molluscs

A mollusc is an animal with no bones. Many molluscs have shells instead. Their eyes are almost always at the top of long stalks.

Mollusc bodies are flexible. They can expand or get smaller when they need to. Most molluscs glide on one flat 'foot' and leave behind a trail of slime. The slime helps them move.

Many molluscs live in the sea. Clams, oysters and octopuses are molluscs. But slugs and land snails live on land.

Land molluscs thrive in plant litter. It hides them from danger and provides shade, moisture and food. Molluscs also live on tree trunks and among stones. Snails with little shells can hide inside the cracks of tree trunks. Snails and slugs love eating the **algae**, mosses and **lichens** they find there.

LESSER BULIN
Merdigera obscura
This snail can climb trees and rocks. Its shell gets dirty. This helps it hide.

DOOR SNAIL
Clausiliidae
This snail lives on dead beech trees. It is found in wild and rainy forests.

CHEESE SNAIL
Helicodonta obvoluta
This mollusc has hairs! Its bristles help camouflage it. They also help cushion it from impact if it falls. It moves between four and seven metres every night. Before winter arrives, it digs itself a shelter in rotten wood.

ROUNDED SNAIL
Discus rotundatus
This snail lives and hides in rotting logs and **humus**. It can take only one snail to start a large colony.

SMALL MAMMALS AND BIRDS

For many mammals like squirrels or weasels, a fallen tree can be a bridge. It helps them to cross a stream without getting their feet wet.

The hollow trunks of dead trees make a cosy winter den for the marten. They are a fine place for wood mice to store food. However, these small animals need to be careful! Foxes know this. They often visit fallen trees in search of prey. But they are sometimes not quick enough to catch the animals hiding there.

Fallen trees are also popular with birds known as jays. The jays like to hide acorns – their favourite food – under or near them. Woodpeckers also visit to find a tasty meal of insect larvae or ants. They use fallen trees to crack open pine cones.

Ⓐ GREAT SPOTTED WOODPECKER
Dendrocopos major

Ⓑ THE WOODPECKER'S WORKSHOP
It is hard to remove seeds from a pine cone without hands. But a woodpecker knows that a fallen tree has perfectly sized holes for the task. The bird finds a good hole and makes it the right size by pecking. Then the woodpecker wedges the pine cone in place. It uses its beak to extract the pine nuts inside.

Ⓒ WEASEL
Mustela nivalis

Ⓓ BANK VOLE
Clethrionomys glareolus
A bank vole is like a hamster that is active during the day. It climbs trees and scrambles among fallen tree trunks, brambles and ferns. The vole is in search of food. It eats fruit, seeds and insects. Its hairy tail is half as long as its body.

GREAT SPOTTED WOODPECKER
Dendrocopos major
The woodpecker has a strong skull. Its skull protects its brain like a helmet would. Its powerful beak hits like a pickaxe. When the woodpecker strikes a tree trunk, its skull and beak move together. This spreads the impact over a wider area. The beak strikes the wood for only a fraction of a second. All of these things prevent damage to the bird's brain.

The woodpecker's tongue is attached to a bone in its throat. When the woodpecker is not using its tongue, the bone is pulled back. The tongue wraps around its skull.

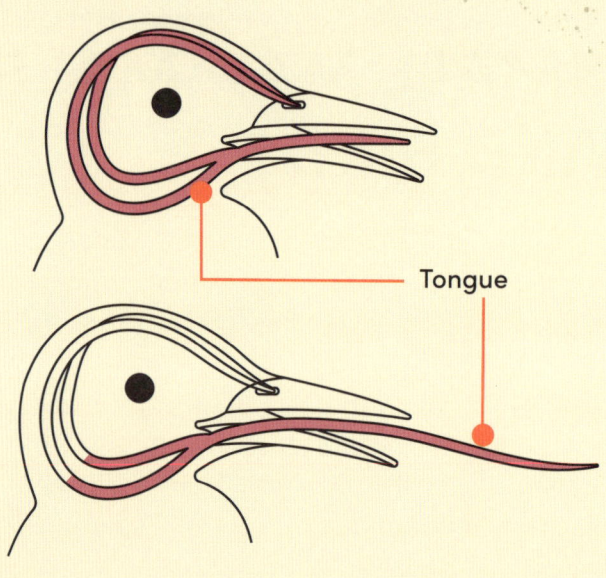
Tongue

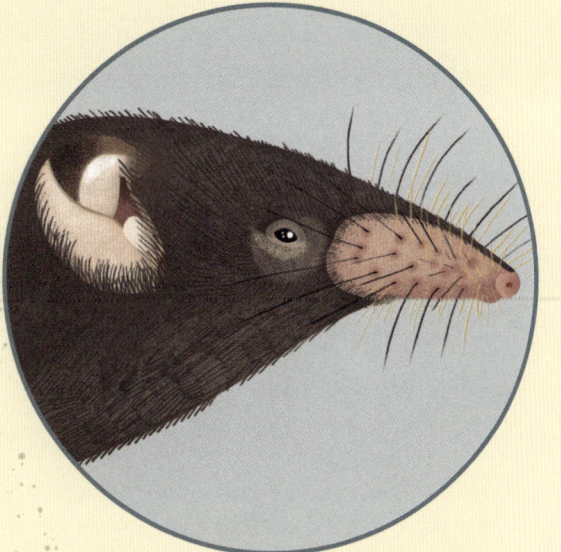

SHREW
Sorex araneus
This shrew likes to find and eat the many insects and earthworms that hide under fallen tree trunks. This small and swift animal is related to the mole and the hedgehog. It has a pointed snout and a keen nose. It has a huge appetite – it wants to eat almost all the time. If a person ate that much, they would be eating the weight of a washing machine in food every day.

BLACKBIRD
Turdus merula
This type of blackbird lives in the forest. Food can be hard to find here, so they have a good tool for foraging. They have slightly longer beaks than the blackbirds we find in our gardens. Their long beaks help them sift through dry leaves. They are hoping to find insects in the plant litter.

Beechnuts

CRESTED TIT
Lophophanes cristatus
This bird has a much smaller beak than the woodpecker. Still, it manages to use it to forage for insects. It can also carve out a nest hole in the soft, rotten wood of trunks that are still standing.

BARBASTELLE BAT
Barbastella barbastellus
The barbastelle bat is so small that it can hide in the tunnels left by large insect larvae. After the insects feed on dead trees, there is space for the bats.

JAY
Garrulus glandarius
This jay is fond of acorns and beechnuts. Like squirrels and mice, it hoards food in hidden places. A fallen tree trunk provides a lot of hiding places. The food will be easy for the jay to find, even after a snow fall. But sometimes a jay (or a squirrel or mouse) forgets where its nuts and seeds are. They might start to grow. In this way, these animals help trees to spread.

WOOD MOUSE
Apodemus sylvaticus
These medium-sized mice dig a burrow under a fallen tree trunk. There, they save acorns and other food for winter.

Hazelnut

Acorn

Bear

Red deer

SNOW

Winter has come. Under the snow, the temperature often stays just above freezing. Fallen tree trunks also offer protection from winter's cold. A snowy forest with rotted wood provides safety for many animals. These include voles and mice. They dig tunnels in the snow and under fallen trees. It also provides a hunting ground for small predators, such as shrews. The shrews explore these tunnels in search of insects and other tasty morsels.

Some plants, such as the blueberry plant, need constant moisture. Snow also guarantees water for those plants.

Winter can be difficult. But animals can still find food above the mantle of snow. They find patches of vegetation growing through the snow. Or they find food that has fallen from the high-up stores of squirrels and birds. A prowling fox is ready to pounce on any small animals caught out in the open.

Passing animals leave tracks in the fresh snow. These tell humans many things about their behaviour. The tracks show the direction they travelled. They tell us how long has passed since they were there. They also show the length of their stride, and perhaps even the animals' intentions.

Roe deer

Lynx

Fox

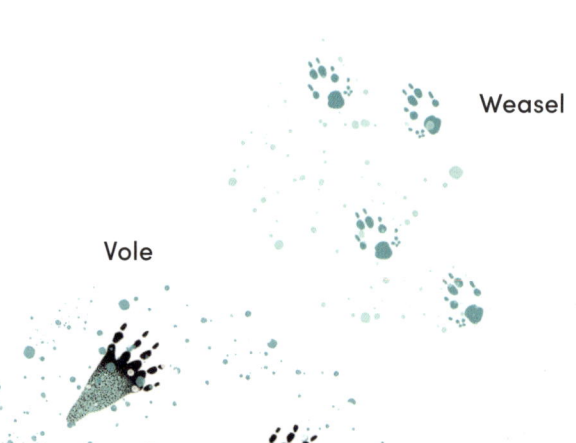
Weasel

Vole

Squirrel

Inside a tree

Inside a tree is a system of long, thin tubes called xylem. Like straws, xylem carry water and minerals from the roots to the branches and leaves. That explains why wood is always slightly moist.

How does a tree decompose?
When a tree first dies, all the twigs and smaller branches fall off. **Fungi** quickly **decompose** them. Next, cracks start to open in the bark. This creates good hiding places for insects and small animals. Eventually, the bark peels away completely. Meanwhile, mosses, **lichens** and small plants grow. They create a miniature forest on the trunk.

Snow, rain, fungi and **bacteria** work together to turn what was hard wood into a soft, reddish, spongy material. Finally, ever-smaller fragments fall away. These turn into **humus** and once again become part of the soil.

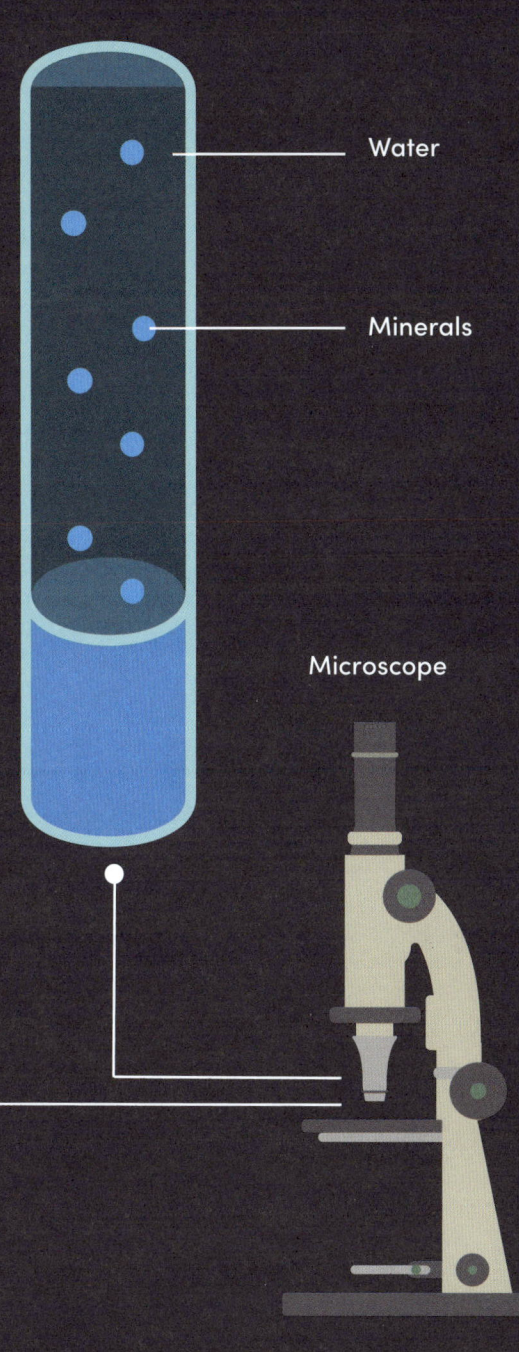

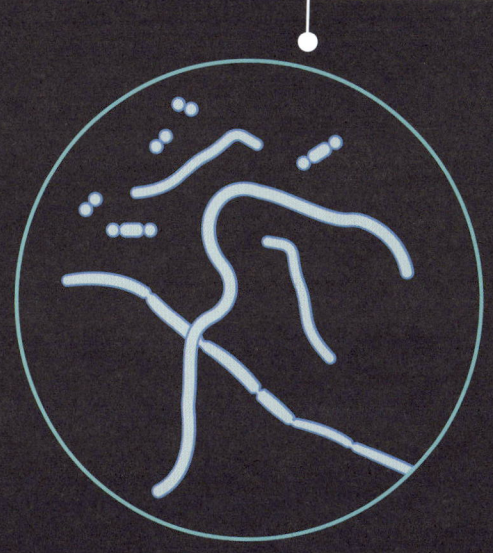

BACTERIA
Bacteria are tiny **organisms** that can't be seen without a microscope. They are not plants, fungi or animals.

The bacteria that live in the fallen tree specialize in transforming wood. They turn it into simpler, more nutritious substances. Plants and fungi can then eat and digest it.

A. SWALLOWTAIL BUTTERFLY
Papilio machaon

B. BERRIES
When spring and summer comes, the forest provides animals with many tasty fruits. We humans can also enjoy some of them. Wild strawberries, blueberries and raspberries are a valuable source of food for bears and wolves, among others.

C. TREE BUMBLEBEE
Bombus hypnorum

FOREST FLOWERS

Winter draws to a close. Each day stretches longer. The air becomes milder, and the sun's heat at last reaches the forest floor. The plants in the undergrowth begin to awaken. Finally, the first leaves and flowers appear.

Bumblebee queens – large insects, covered with tufts of hair – scour the area. They search for early flowers. They might also look for a good place to build a new colony. Reptiles and amphibians emerge from their shelters. They come from among the rocks or under the trunk of our fallen tree. Spiders and insects resume their deadly game of hide-and-seek.

As spring progresses, the flowers multiply. The air fills with more and more pollinating insects. They fly from flower to flower in search of nectar and food. They bring tiny pollen grains from one plant to another as they go. This will enable the plants to produce fruits and seeds. Some pollinators lay eggs in holes and tunnels they find in trees. They leave food nearby for their hungry larvae to find when they hatch.

The flowers of the clearing

Our tree created a sunny clearing when it fell. This open space has less moisture than the surrounding forest. It provides a home for plants that love the sun and can withstand heat.

Some plants prefer less light and more moisture. Those grow on the edges of the clearing in the shade of trees.

SNOWDROP
Galanthus nivalis
This plant loves cool meadows, but it's easy to find elsewhere. Look in the moist **humus** near fallen tree trunks.

LIVERLEAF
Hepatica nobilis
The liverleaf is easily identified by its leaves. Each leaf is divided into three wide sections. Liverleaf blooms at the end of winter, with flowers that are pink when they open. After a few hours they turn blue, violet or purple. This plant grows well in cool humus. It can be found near old fallen tree trunks.

TOUCH-ME-NOT BALSAM
Impatiens noli-tangere
The Latin scientific name for this plant means 'unwilling to endure, do not touch'. It produces small fruit that burst open when touched. This scatters seeds everywhere. Bumblebees and other pollinators love this plant. It has yellow flowers with long spurs. It can be found in areas with slightly moist soil.

OAK FERN
Gymnocarpium dryopteris
Ferns are plants that produce neither flowers nor fruit. To reproduce, they create tiny spores instead of seeds. They live in shady, sheltered spots where the soil is rich in humus.

WOOD SORREL
Oxalis acetosella
This plant needs a lot of humus. For this reason, it often lives near old stumps and fallen trunks. It is one of the earliest species to flower in the spring.

LARGE ANIMALS

Forests around the world are home to many large animals. In this forest in Europe, many different animals will visit our fallen tree.

Lynxes only feed on the prey they catch. These include rodents, foxes, roe deer and even large red deer. These beautiful, rare mammals roam large territories. They use their acute sense of sight, smell and hearing to hunt. Like domestic cats, they are excellent jumpers and climbers.

Wolves live and hunt in family groups called packs. They howl to communicate. Like lynxes, they inhabit large territories and travel long distances. And like dogs, wolves sometimes eat fruit, especially if meat is scarce. They use fallen trees as hiding places. They also use them as obstacles to slow down possible predators. These include humans, lynxes and bears.

Brown bears are omnivores that eat little meat. They dig into and move fallen tree trunks. They are in search of whatever food they can find underneath, such as a nice ant nest. Bears often leave claw marks on trees. Badgers leave claw marks, too. They are constantly foraging for food such as earthworms, ripe fruit and insect larvae. They dig for these in the wood.

A playground

A fallen tree is a wonderful playground for the young of many species. Wolf cubs from a nearby den play among their branches while waiting for the adults to return. Bear cubs also play here. They must be big and strong by the time they reach adulthood. If they aren't, they won't be able to move boulders and logs in search of food. To get stronger, they use fallen trunks as a kind of gym. Lynx kittens happily use the branches and roots of a fallen tree, too. It is a springboard for their games.

A danger

For large herbivores such as deer, a freshly fallen tree can be an unexpected supply of fresh leaves. This is food that would otherwise be too high to reach. However, they can also be a serious danger. It could block a deer from escaping a predator. Knowing escape routes and when to jump can save the lives of these fast creatures.

THE FOREST AND US

The forest is a place of constant discovery.

Among the whispering trees we can find signs of so much animal life. We see the remains of the meal of an owl, squirrel or woodpecker. There are signs that animals have passed by, such as tracks left on the path or in a muddy puddle.

We can find out more about animals and their habits – where they hide, or when they emerge from their shelters. We can find out how they move, and how they communicate. We can learn to recognize birds by listening to their songs.

We can marvel at the incredible variety of **fungi** and their important role in the forest. For example, think about the way they transform dead wood into new forms. We can admire their varied colours, their many shapes, the places they love to live.

And what about us? What evidence do we leave in the forest when we pass by? If we are responsible, we leave just our footprints. Only people without respect for the forest leave behind rubbish. Plastic, glass and other man-made materials have no place in the forest. If we want to do something for the forest, we should take a bag with us and collect any rubbish we find.

MESSY IS BEST

Plant litter looks messy. But it makes the soil fertile and supports life of all kinds. A neat and tidy forest could not thrive.

The same applies to our gardens. Yet, when many people think of an ideal garden, they dream of a beautifully trimmed lawn. They picture plants spaced well apart. There are no weeds or overgrown plants. Leaves, grass clippings and fallen twigs are all removed. There are not many insects. Those have been killed with insecticides.

However, if we changed our habits and let nature take its course, we would be amazed.

A compost bin for organic household waste would fill up with earthworms. The compost, when spread on our gardens, would improve the soil. It would strengthen the plants. Wood, clippings and leaves on the ground would become a winter home for insects. As the plant litter **decomposed**, the nutrients it contained would return to the soil. The soil would become more fertile, like forest soil. Wild flowers would grow in the spring. These would feed pollinators. Plants left to themselves would produce fruit and seeds. And the fruit and seeds would attract many different birds.

New balances would form. They would give us the chance to observe and learn.

GLOSSARY

ALGA (ALGAE)
A small plant that does not have leaves or roots.

BACTERIA
Bacteria are tiny organisms. They are not plants, fungi or animals. They can't be seen without a microscope.

DECOMPOSE
To transform dead leaves, wood, and animal or plant remains into simpler substances. These can be used as nutrients by other living things.

FUNGI (FUNGUS)
Organisms made up of thin white strands called hyphae. The only part of a fungus that we see above ground is its fruiting body.

HUMUS
A dark and very fertile soil. It's mainly made of pieces of decomposed trees and plants.

LICHEN
An organism made up of a fungus and an alga. The fungus and alga support each other in symbiosis.

ORGANISM
A living thing, such as a plant, animal or bacteria.

PARASITE
A living thing that takes food and energy from another without giving anything in return.

SYMBIOSIS
The coexistence of two or more different species. The relationship benefits both or all of them.

NEW LIFE FROM DEAD WOOD

The tree that fell in the forest first grew from a seed. The forest is full of seeds. Many of them are eaten or hidden by animals. Some are lost or left in hiding places, forgotten. Others fall into cracks in the earth or the trunks of dead trees. Those few seeds that find fertile soil can begin their lives as tiny shoots and frail seedlings. They slowly gain strength, height and width, thriving in their mossy home.

When a tree falls and a new clearing is created, everything changes. This is a long-awaited moment for many species. It is the start of a race among plants to see which ones can reach the light first.

The forest will eventually reclaim the clearing, but sooner or later another will form. The cycle will begin anew.

Phaidon Press Limited
2 Cooperage Yard
London E15 2QR

Phaidon Press Inc.
111 Broadway
New York, NY 10006

Phaidon SARL
55, rue Traversière
75012 Paris

phaidon.com

This edition © 2025 Phaidon Press Limited
First published in Italian as *Caduto. La seconda vita degli alberi*
© 2023 Cocai Books
Rovereto (TN), Italy
Concept and illustrations by Valentina Gottardi
Text by Maciej Michno and Danio Miserocchi
Scientific supervision by Danio Miserocchi

Translation rights arranged through Syllabes Agency, France

ISBN 978 1 83729 028 4 (UK edition)
002-0625

A CIP catalogue record for this book is available from the British Library.

All rights reserved. No part of this publication may be reproduced, stored in a retrieval system or transmitted, in any form or by any means, electronic, mechanical, photocopying, recording or otherwise, without the written permission of Phaidon Press Limited.

Printed in China

Commissioning Editor: Alice-May Bermingham
Project Editor: Rachel Craig-McFeely
Production Controller: Rebecca Price
Design: Laura Hambleton

Special thanks to Cecilia Michno for making one of the illustrations in this book very special.

*To my father
– VG*